IRISH FOLKLORE

BRÍD MAHON

MERCIER PRESS

CONTENTS

1

ONCE UPON A TIME

What little we know of the story of pre-Christian Ireland is found in the archaeological remains which have come down to us from early days. The great passage tombs in the Boyne Valley, Newgrange, Knowth and Howth are decorated with whorls, spirals and lines – the finest megalithic art in Ireland. The burial sites are older than Stonehenge and much older than the Pyramids of Egypt. The Irish remains include a circle of standing stones in Cork where pagan people worshipped their gods, cooking pits where the legendary band of heroes called the *Fianna* feasted after a day's hunting, a necklace of amber beads buried with a Stone Age prince, bronze cauldrons, earthenware pots, axeheads, knives and bronze pins. The radiantly beautiful gold collar known as the Gleninsheen gorget, some 3,000 years old, was found in a rabbit burrow by a young boy in 1932, and the exquisite Ardagh chalice, a solid and airy, bold and restrained artefact dating to the end of the seventh century, was discovered, along with four brooches and a bronze cup, by a Limerick boy digging potatoes in the prehistoric fort of Ardagh in 1868.

Side by side with the artifacts go the sagas, traditions and folklore dealing with the remote past, when gods and heroes walked the earth. These tales are the chief source of knowledge of the pagan Irish. Very little is known of these people's religion save that they believed in a happy underworld: a Hy-Brasil set in the western seas, where mortals were sometimes allowed to visit – a place where, in the words of the poet W. B. Yeats:

> *Nobody gets old and crafty and wise,*
> *Nobody gets old and bitter of tongue.*

On that lost island, time had a different meaning, as Oisín of the *Fianna* discovered when he went with Niamh of the golden hair to Tír na nÓg, 'the Land of the Young', riding a snow-white steed over the waves. He remained there for three years and returned home to Ireland to find that, in this absence, 300 years had elapsed and all his old companions of the *Fianna* were long since dead.

There is no trace of who the authors of these ancient sagas were; indeed no single writer may have been responsible for them. Possibly they were an amalgam of remembered stories, taboos, customs, traditions and clan or family histories, interwoven with Celtic mythology and folklore and handed down by word of mouth for countless generations.

The Red Branch cycle, which consists of a group of romantic tales, is probably the oldest of the epic tales. The traditional date of the cycle is 100 AD, and the state of civilisation portrayed in it is pagan. The stories tell of the standing army of Red Branch Knights; of Maeve, Queen of Connacht, and her husband Ailill; and of Deirdre and the ill-fated sons of Usnech. They describe the marvellous palace of Emain Macha, with its great bronze door and walls of carved wood; they tell of the destruction of Da

Derga's Hostel on the road to Bohernabreena, County Dublin, and of the Princess Étain, who was turned into a golden butterfly through the jealousy of a rival goddess and was reborn in Ireland as a girl-child.

One of the beliefs of the pagan Irish, as evidenced by the early literature, was in re-incarnation, or the transmigration of souls. The story of the hero who dies dishonoured and is reborn many times – as a salmon, a stag, a hound and a great boar roaming the forest – until his final reincarnation as a man, when he redeems himself and is restored to favour among the gods, is a common one.

The Ulster cycle has for its central story the *Táin Bó Cuailgne* (*The Cattle Raid of Cooley*). One man, Cúchulainn, stands alone at the Pass of Ulster defending the province against the army of Maeve, Queen of Connacht, while his companions lie in an enchanted slumber. The saga was first written down from oral sources at Clonmacnoise, the monastic city founded by St Ciarán in the sixth century. Set in the heart of Ireland and on the banks of the Shannon, Clonmacnoise attracted students from all over Ireland.

In the 600 years that followed its foundation, Clonmacnoise was plundered eighteen times – by Vikings, Munstermen and roving bands of robbers – but each time it was lovingly rebuilt by the monks. Today the few archaeological artifacts that remain there include the ninth-century stone cross known as the South Cross, the Cross of the Scriptures or West Cross, the remains of the foundation churches, St Ciarán's grave and the Nuns' Church, which was built by Dervorgilla, Princess of Meath and mistress of Dermot McMurrough. He, it is said, precipitated the Norman invasion in 1169.

According to legend, the early Irish saints had as their pets the fox, the cat, the badger, the boar, the wren, the dog and the cat. Even the humble fly was sure of their protection. Ciarán had a favourtie dun cow, and when the animal died the monks preserved its skin as a holy relic. Tradition has it that the *Táin Bó Cuailgne* was first written down at Clonmacnoise, in the early seventh century, on the vellum from the skin of Ciarán's beloved cow. In time the story passed again into folklore, until the twelfth century, when we find an unknown author using the mangled version of *The Book of the Dun Cow* to commit the tale to writing once more.

The finest of all the Ulster stories – and one which has passed from oral literature to the written word and back again many times – is *The Exile of the Sons of Usnech*. It is the earliest form of the love motif in Irish literature, the theme of which later became famous in the story of Tristan and Iseult. The background to the *Táin* is the long war between Connacht and Ulster brought about by the ill-fated elopement of Deirdre (who is betrothed to the High King Conor) and Naoise, one of the three sons of Usnech. A druid had foretold at Deirdre's birth that she would be the most beautiful woman in Ireland and would bring ruin to the men of Ulster.

For half a year Naoise and Deirdre travelled around Ireland from Assaroe to the south-west and to Howth and north again to escape Conor's vengeance. Harried and hunted, the lovers were not able to spend more than one night in any bed, nor were they able to eat more than one meal at any table. They fled to Scotland with Naoise's two brothers, Ardan and Ainle, and settled in Glen Etive, in the hollow of Ben Cruachan, where the waters run deep. There they were happy for a time. But like many exiles they longed for home, and after a couple of years they returned to Ireland under the protection of one of the Red Branch Knights, Fergus Mac Roy. No sooner had they reached Ireland than the sons of Usnech were slain by order of King Conor. After that Deirdre submitted to Conor but she was never again known to smile.

To punish her, the High King decided to share her with Eogan Mac Durthacht, King of Fernmag, the man who had slain Naoise, and she set out with the pair of them for the Fair of Macha. She rode in a chariot while the other two rode on horseback, one on either side of her. 'Between me and Eogan you are a sheep eyeing two rams,' Conor mocked her, but Deirdre had sworn that two men alive in the world together would never have her. At a turn in the road a huge stone blocked the chariot. Deidre threw herself against the rock so that it shattered her head, and when Conor reached her she was dead, thus fulfilling the druid's prophecy. Fergus Mac Roy was so enraged with King Conor that he attacked the palace of Emain Macha and burnt it to the ground, then fled to Connacht, where for ten years he kept up incessant raids on Ulster.

Stories such as these fill in the background and preserve the memory of a real world that vanished at the beginning of history. We are an island people, and for more than 1,000 years the old ways continued uninterrupted. A long tradition of native learning, lore and legend, sagas and poetry had grown up in the Druidic schools preserved by the *file*, or poet, by oral transmission; some of these tales continue to be told down to our own times. Folk customs and folk beliefs were part of everyday life, and the 'other world' was no further away than the nearest fairy fort or thorn bush.

2

THE COMING OF PATRICK

History is said to have begun in Ireland in the fifth century, when the boy Patrick, abducted from a wealthy Roman villa, was captured and sold as a slave-shepherd to Miliucc, a petty chieftain who ruled over the area between Lough Neagh and the Slemish Mountains in County Antrim. After six years Patrick managed his escape and returned home but he never forgot the people amongst whom he had been enslaved.

In his writings he tells of a dream or vision he had in which a man named Victorious he knew in Ireland visits him, holding countless letters. He hands one, headed 'The Voice of the Irish', to Patrick. As Patrick reads, he hears the voices of countless people crying out, 'We beg you to come and walk among us once more.' He awakens in tears. His dream gives him no peace of mind and so in the year 432 we find him returning to the land where he had endured bitter years in hunger and loneliness to minister as a bishop. The next thirty years of his life were to be spent converting the Irish to Christianity, and according to legend in all that time only one man was slain in the country. Thanks to Patrick's teaching, people learnt to read and write, first in Latin and later in their native tongue, Irish. Patrick was no scholar but a man of the people; perhaps this is one reason he was so successful in his mission.

By the sixth century, monastic scholars had set about compiling a written record of the Irish people and their origins. Their guiding purpose was to accommodate this tradition within the framework provided by the Bible and early Christian historians. Everything was grist to their mill; these early scribes and monks copied down all they knew of oral literature and tradition as well as the ancient, time-worn tales of Greece and Rome. In *The Book of Leinster*, which contains an elaborate version of the *Táin Bó Cuailgne*, the scribe wrote down in Irish the earlier oral bardic formula, 'A blessing on everyone who will memorise the *Táin* as it is written down and not put any other form on it.'

Perhaps the most charming picture we possess of a scribe at work is contained in a poem called 'Pangur Bán'. which was slipped into a ninth-century manuscript. The translation by Robin Flower begins: 'I and Pangur Bán my cat/'Tis a like task we are at.' The cat hunts mice: the scribe hunts words, both contentedly, 'When at home we sit and find/Entertainment in our mind.'

One of the most popular of the epic tales is the Fenian cycle, which gets its name from the band of legendary heroes called the *Fianna*. Fionn Mac Cumhail was the chief and the wisest man in Ireland, due to the fact that he had got the first taste of the magic salmon of Assaroe. The Irish annalists reckoned that the *Fianna* lived in the third century AD, in the reign of Cormac Mac Art and about 200 years after Cúchulainn and the Red Branch Knights. They spent most of their time hunting, shooting and fishing and had the kind of adventures the ordinary person might only dream about.

Legend tells us that Saint Patrick ordered his monks to write down the adventures of Fionn and the *Fianna* lest they be forgotten. According to the stories that have come down to us, he was said to have baptised the last of the *Fianna*. When he put the question, 'Was your chieftain, Fionn Mac Cumhail, a good master?' Caoilte's proud reply was, 'Were but the brown leaf which the wood sheds from it gold, were but the white billows silver, Fionn would have given it all away.'

Folk memory is tenacious, and 1,500 years later we find an extartordinary link with the remote past. In 1932, Robin Flower, the English writer and scholar, on holiday on the Great Blasket Island off the west coast of Kerry, met an old man, who could neither read nor write, digging potatoes in a field. The old man laid down his spade and began to recite from memory Ossianic poetry he had heard as a boy from a *seanchaí*. After a little while, he changed from poetry to prose and told a long story of the adventures of Fionn and his companions. Flower said later, 'I listened spellbound and it came to me suddenly that there on the last inhabited piece of European land, looking out to the Atlantic horizon, I was hearing the oldest living tradition in the British Isles.'

When the Viking pirates descended in their long-prowed ships to ransack and burn monasteries and churches in the Ireland of the ninth and tenth centuries, only a few manuscript fragments survived their raids. Two hundred years later a number of great manuscript compilations had been pieced together; between them these compilations preserved a wealth of varied material relating to Irish traditional lore and the Irish past. Some manuscripts were compiled from earlier sources, but many were lost or destroyed in the wars and plantations in the centuries that followed.

The most important of what remains of the great folio manuscripts are *The Book of Leinster*, preserved in Trinity College Dublin; a manuscript whose title is lost and which is housed in the Bodleian Library in Oxford; *The Leabhar Breac*, or 'Speckled Book'; *The Book of Ballymote*; and of the course *The Book of the Dun Cow*, which is preserved in the Royal Irish Academy in Dublin.

Through the vicissitudes of history, tales once told in kingly halls by bards and poets were kept alive orally by fishermen helping each other to stay awake in the still reaches of the night, by itinerant labourers and craftsmen travelling the roads, in sessions of storytelling around the fire and at patterns held at holy wells and bonfires on the eve of the four ancient festivals: St Brigid's Eve, May Eve, St John's Eve and Hallowe'en.

It is true to say that Patrick and those monks and clerics who came after him never troubled themselves about eradicating pagan influences, which is why customs and traditions connected with the year's fectivals continued for countless generations. Until the Victorian era, the Irish church turned a blind eye to the bacchanalian drinking, dancing and various sexual indiscretions which took place at fertility festivals. One such festival, Puck Fair in Killorglin, County Kerry, has lasted down to the present, being held each August. At the heart of the festival is a magnificent he-goat which presides on a platform high over the town for three days and three nights.

In Irish folk tradition *'Imbolc'* (the word associated with milk, butter and cheese) was the ancient name for the feast of Brigid, 1 February. It was the turning point of the year: winter was past and a feast was held in every house on this night. Generally milk was scarce at this time of year but the thrifty housewife usually saved some butter for the supper celebration. If there was a neighbour who had little or no milk, a can of fresh buttermilk with a lump of butter on top was sent to that person in order that no one should go short.

In pagan times Brigid was once widely worshipped not alone in Ireland but also amongst the Continental Celts. In Christian times 1 February was celebrated in Ireland as the feast of St Brigid, who lived in the fifth and sixth centuries and was abbess of the great monastery of Kildare, ruling over nuns and priests alike. Many of the miracles attributed to her and stories about her are folk memories of the myths that once surrounded the goddess Brigid.

May Day, or Beltaine, was distinguished by bonfires, maypoles and sexual licence. The fairies, or people of the *sí*, changed residence on this night and witches stole butter and cream from their neighbours.

St John's Eve, 23 June, was generally observed as midsummer's day. At dawn cattle were driven through the *gríosach* or ashes of the bonfire to prevent their being 'overlooked'. Herbs gathered at this time of year were especialy powerful. St John's Wort, *Hypericum*, was known as the fairy herb because of its curative properties. Lúnasa, celebrated on the Sunday which fell closest to 1 August, was the day the people climbed the heights, picked the first fruit of the season and danced for joy. This early pagan custom is observed to this day by the pilgrims who climb the holy mountain of Croagh Patrick in County Mayo.

The ancient festival of winter known as Samhain was kept on 1 November. In the Christian calendar it is the Feast of All Saints. The vigil of the feast is Hallowe'en, which has lasted longest, not only in Ireland but across the Atlantic. Colcannon (made with kale or green cabbage, mashed potatoes and chopped onions and milk) was the favourite supper dish for

Hallowe'en and was followed by a feast of apples, nuts and barm brack. Hunger and famine were symbolically banished by throwing a cake of bread against the door.

The eve of Samhain, or Hallowe'en, was the night the fairies opened their forts and moved to their winter quarters. Woe betide any mortal who ventured abroad on that night. Unmarried boys and girls cast spells and chanted incantations to see what partner the future would bring them.

Hallowe'en corresponded with the ancient Feast of the Dead. Candles were lit in windows and it was believed that the dead were released from the 'other world' at midnight to return to their homes, to eat the food spread on the table by their kith and kin and to warm themselves at the good fires left down. In Christian belief the Day of the Dead has been moved to 2 November and is called the Feast of All Souls.

The winter solstice, 21 December, is another night the dead were believed to return to earth. This belief goes back 5,000 years or more and can be witnessed when at daybreak the first fingers of the rising sun creep along the passage, eventually lighting up first the cremation basis and then the whole of the burial chamber at Newgrange in the Boyne Valley.

Times have changed. We are at the beginning of the third millennium AD, and our traditions, folklore and festivals of yesteryear are nothing but memories. Yet despite what was saved we shall never know how much we have lost. The manuscript and oral literature preserved to us are but haunting fragments of an immense body of literature which perished in consequence of both the downfall of the old aristocratic Gaelic world in the disastrous wars of the seventeenth century and the gradual decay of the Irish language during the last 200 years over almost the whole of Ireland. What remained was kept alive in the oral literature and traditions of a vanquished people. The archives and library of the Department of Irish Folklore at University College Dublin bear testimony to this in the thousands of manuscripts, books, tapes and items of photographic material gathered there. This collection is a moving tribute to the men and

women, living in quiet places, who gave so
much to the country's folklore.

3

THE GAELIC STORYTELLER

The art of storytelling in Ireland is very old. In early times the storyteller, like the poet, ranked next to the king in importance. The storyteller sat at the royal table, wore a coat of many colours and owned herds of cattle: all of these things were indications of his wealth and importance.

Early Irish society was monarchical. The king reigned over his people as judge in peace and leader in war, but he was not the lawgiver. Laws were adopted by the people at assemblies called *aontaí*, and when the serious business of giving judgements and framing new laws was over, jugglers and musicians entertained the company and the storyteller came into his own. He related epic poems and traditional stories of ancient heroes, kings and knights and told of the power of the great Crom Cruach, of Nuada of the silver hand, of Bress the champion and of Dagda the builder. He also gave graphic accounts of the early invasions.

A favourite story tells of the second battle of Moytura between early settlers – the ill-visaged Fomorians, whose leader was Balor of the Evil Eye – and the beautiful Tuatha Dé Danaan, under their leader Lugh. Balor's eye never opened save on a battlefield and had a poisonous power. If an army looked at that eye, though they were many thousand they were doomed to die. But at the Battle of Moytura, Lugh saved the day by casting a slingstone which carried the evil eye through the back of Balor's head. The slingstone and the eye fell on the host of the ill-favoured Fomorians; they were destroyed and the battle was won by the magical Tuatha Dé Danaan. Later this race would in turn be defeated by the Celts. According to folklore, sooner than leave the Ireland they loved the Tuatha Dé Danaan took up residence in fairy forts and in the hollow hills – and are there to this very day.

We know of course that the *Lebor Gabala* (*'Book of Invasions'*) is largely make-believe – or rather an adapted and embroidered version of earlier stories and legends. Lugh and Balor, Bress the Champion, the Daghda and Nuada of the silver hand were not real people at all but the gods of the pagan Irish. Most early civilisations believed that there were many gods who had created the world long ago. They thought the gods were supermen but with the same kinds of passions that humans felt.

It had long been the storyteller's function to preserve traditional lore in relation to places, families, events, customs and laws. Some of the stories were very old and had travelled the known world. These were described as international folk tales; parallels with them are to be found in many countries. Perhaps the oldest known international folk tale to survive in Ireland was first discovered on Egyptian papyrus 3,260 years ago. It is entitled 'Ao Mhic an Bhradáin agus Ó Mhic an Bhradáin' ('Hugh and O, the Two Sons of the Salmon'). When the boys grow to manhood the elder is turned to stone by an enchantress but in the end is rescued by his brother. Another ancient international tale is that of Cinderella (in Ireland she is known as

'Ashy Pet'). Such tales were probably brought here by early settlers – perhaps by travellers, traders or fishermen – and were still being told by storytellers down to the middle of the twentieth century.

For well over 1,000 years the official story-teller continued to be an important member of the community. Even the incursions of the Norsemen in the ninth and tenth centuries and the Norman invasion of the twelfth century did little to change the old way of life. Storytellers were still welcomed in keep and castle, in fortified towns and at the seats of Irish princes and chieftains.

With the downfall of the old Gaelic order after the Battle of Kinsale and the flight of the earls of Tyrone and Tyrconnell in the early seventeenth century, the traditional storyteller lost his noble patrons and was forced to make a living amongst the common herd. Tales that had once delighted Irish princes, Viking pirates and Norman barons were now heard only around the hearths of small farmers and humble fisher-men.

Some of the great storytellers knew hundreds

of tales, many of which might take a week in the telling. To be a good storyteller and hold the attention of your audience required skill as an actor as well as a phenomenal memory. Many storytellers could neither read nor write but their language was clear and vigorous and had in it the stuff of literature. A good storyteller's mind was a storehouse of tradition of all kinds: intricate hero-tales, historical anecdotes, proverbs, rhymes and riddles, prayers and incantations, folk medicine and music. The 'Derry Air' (popularly known as 'Danny Boy') is only one example of the storyteller's lore. We shall never know who composed this exquisite traditional air.

People exchanged stories while going about their daily tasks: digging potatoes, making hay, mending nets or waiting to bring in the catch. Lodging houses and wake houses were centres for storytellers. Travelling tailors, masons, *spailpíní* and beggars going the roads carried stories from one village to the next.

As a rule, storytelling took place between Hallowe'en and the end of March. In every townland in the district there was at least one house to which the neighbours would resort during the nights of winter. Storytellers were loath to recount folk tales at their own hearth and preferred to go to a *tigh áirneáil*, or house of welcome, as it was known. In the congenial atmosphere of such a house their performances were appreciated by the grown-up audience. In return for the hospitality and storytelling, the guests attended to the simple wants of their host, bringing gifts of turf for the fire, a griddle loaf of bread, a clutch of eggs and occasionally a bottle of well-matured poteen. When the house was full to the door, the man of the house would fill his pipe with tobacco, take a few puffs and then pass it to the storyteller. After that the pipe went the rounds from one to another. By the time the last man had enjoyed his smoke, all the current topics of interest had been discussed and the storytelling could now begin.

Many of the great storytellers had first heard their tales as children, listening to their elders while hiding under the kitchen table or crouching on the stairs leading to the loft above the kitchen, where they shared their sleeping quarters with fishing tackle and maybe the family dog or domestic fowl. They would absorb folk tales that were longer that the modern blockbuster and could retell them word for word half a century later.

It would appear that there was a taboo on the telling of heroic tales during the daytime. 'Whistling at night and *fiannaíocht* by day' were considered unlucky, according to the proverb. The recital of Ossianic hero-tales was, almost without exception, confined to men. A woman *fiannaí* or a crowing hen was unlucky and something to be avoided.

While women did not as a rule take part in the storytelling, not a word of the tale escaped them, and if necessary they did not hesitate to correct the speaker. The storyteller would begin a tale with the magic words *'Fadó, fadó'* or 'Once upon a time in a land far, far away.' Today in the ever-popular science-fiction movie *Star Wars*, flashed across the screen almost word for word is the same dramatic opening: 'Once upon a time in a galaxy far, far away . . . ' In both the ancient sagas and the modern story and screen-play, we find the hero engaging in gigantic battles and perilous adventures, always against

Cooking pit of the legendary band of
warriors the Fianna

Bricriu's Feast, where Cúchulainn was confirmed as the greatest hero in Ireland

A hermit praises the abundance of
good food in Ireland

During the reign of the high king Conaire the Great it
was said that there was oakmast up to
the knees to fatten the pigs

A nineteenth-century bride en route
to her country wedding

A traditional Irish dancing session

impossible odds. Good invariably triumphs over evil in the early hero-tales. Meanwhile, sexual encounters were taken as a matter of course. The young man beds the girl on the first night they meet, then takes off on his adventures. Nine months later she gives birth to a child.

The 'runs' that appeared here and there in the story gave the storyteller time to draw breath and gather his thoughts for the description of the next adventure the hero would meet:

Away and away he rode by hills and hollows and thorny ways, by green valleys, shimmering lochs and singing streams, by fairy raths and the Great Plains of Dreams, farther than I could tell you and twice the distance you could tell me.

It was usual for the storyteller to finish his tale with the wedding of the hero and the girl with whom he had fallen in love. This called for another favourite run, with which the listeners, who had heard it many times before, would join in:

They returned home and held a feast that lasted seven days and seven nights and the last day was better than the first. There were 700 guests at the short table, 800 at the round table and 1,000 in the grand hall. I was there and heard the whole story but got no present except shoes of paper and stockings of buttermilk, and these a herder stole from me in crossing the mountains.

At this the man of the house would stand up to show that the night's storytelling was at an end and, crossing himself, would say the prayer:

May the company and myself be 7,000 times better off a year from today. And the blessing of God and the Church on the souls of the dead. Amen.

One of the few female storytellers was Peig Sayers (1873–1958), who is buried in the graveyard at Dunquin, County Kerry, in sight of the Great Blasket Island, where she spent her married life. Readers of Robin Flower's charming book *The Western Island* will recall the tribute paid to this remarkable woman, who might have been a great actress had she lived in another time and place.

Peig, who met her husband-to-be, Pádraig Ó Guithín, for the first time on the day they were married (it was a case of love at first sight), kept her maiden name of Sayers all her married life, as was the folk tradition. Seosamh Ó Dála, folklore collector with the Irish Folklore Commission, obtained 375 tales from her – not surprising when one remembers that her father, Tomás Sayers, was a renowned *seanchaí* himself. He gave stories to the American folklorist and writer Jeremiah Curtin (1838–1906); these were published by Curtin in Boston in 1890 under the title *Myths and Folklore of Ireland*.

Tadhg Ó Murchú, whose twenty-three-year career as a full-time folklorist with the Irish Folklore Commission ended in 1958 with his early death, has left a description of one of the last great storytellers. He met the eighty-five-year-old Kerry *seanchaí* for the first time in 1935. Had Ó Murchú come even five years earlier, the old man said, he would have had a tale for every day of the year, but alas his memory was not what it had once been.

This old man was rare in that he could speak and read both Irish and English. Tadhg Ó Murchú describes him as follows:

> His piercing eyes are on my face as, immersed in the story, he puts his very soul into the telling. He uses a great deal of gesticulation and by the movement of his body, hands and head tries to convey hate and anger, fear and humour, like an actor in a play. He raises his voice at certain passages, at other times it becomes almost a whisper. He speaks fairly fast but his enunciation is at all times clear. I have never met anyone who told his tales with more artistry and effect than this very fine old storyteller.

The advent of radio and television put an end to the art of the storyteller. By the mid-1960s the last of them had gone *ar slí na fírinne*, or 'the way of truth'. Stories that had enthralled our ancestors for aeons were no more than a memory.

Only a few fragments of the oral literature once found in the greater part of Ireland have been preserved. A few scholars devoted as much time as they could to the work of collection. Patrick Kennedy in the ninetheenth century gathered a number of tales from the Wexford–Carlow border. Sir William Wilde, the distinguished eye-and-ear surgeon and father of Oscar Wilde, spent his summers on the shores of Lough Corrib. His holiday villa was called Moytura, after the two great mythical battles that were said to have taken place in the area. While tending the local people, he wrote down their lore and legends. When they attempted to pay him for his services with butter, a cake of soda bread, a fowl, a length of tweed or a gansey they had knitted, he bargained instead for a ghost story, a folk tale, an account of the *Fianna* or a story of the ancient gods. He published these stories in a volume entitled *Ancient Legends, Mystic Charms and Superstitions*.

But the hidden Ireland of the Gaelic-speaking world, with its wealth of tales and traditions, remained largely unknown until it was discovered by Douglas Hyde (1860–1949), who was to become the first president of Ireland. Due to a childhood illness, Hyde, who was the son of a Church of Ireland rector, spent his formative years at his home in Frenchpark, County Roscommon, where his companions were the barefooted children of the local peasantry. From their parents and grandparents he heard his first tales and thereafter everything he did and wrote was imbued with his burning passion for the Irish language and Irish folklore. He founded the Gaelic League, a movement for the revival of the Irish language, in 1893 and published collections of folk tales, rhymes, riddles and traditional songs that he had gathered.

A man of great charm and vision, Hyde was a friend of the poet W. B. Yeats. Like Yeats, he fell in love at first sight with the legendary Maud Gonne, who was described by the London *Times* as the most beautiful woman in Europe. He gave her lessons in Irish and tried to interest her in folklore, but as she was to say later: 'Douglas Hyde never succeeded in making me an Irish speaker, any more than I in making him a revolutionary.'

In 1908 Hyde was appointed the first professor of modern Irish when the National University of Ireland was established. One of his students, a red-haired young man from Cushendall, County Antrim, named Séamus Ó Duilearga (1899–1980) was so fired with his professor's passion that he set out on his own odyssey in the spring of 1923 – a journey that was to lead him to Cill Rialaigh, Ballinskelligs, in the barony of Iveragh in County Kerry. Here he met Seán Ó Conaill, a gentle and dignified man of seventy years, whose storehouse of tales and traditions Ó Duilearga wrote down at intervals over an eight-year period. It was to save the legacy of this vanishing world that he founded the Irish Folklore Commission in 1935. He became its honorary director and the first professor of Irish folklore. Séamus Ó Duilearga was not only an inspired collector but was to become the friend, champion and chronicler of the last of the Gaelic storytellers.

4

THE UNSEEN WORLD

In Irish tradition the unseen world is all around us, and stories of magicians, hags, ghosts and fairies were the currency of everyday life. The 'invisible folk' were everywhere. They might be glimpsed going by in a whirlwind, dancing under the moonlight or selling and buying cattle at a mart of a fair. (The cattle they sold invariably returned home to the fairy forts, while the gold they paid for the cattle turned to dust in the hands of the human buyer.)

The people of the *sí*, or the 'Good People' or 'Gentle Folk', as the fairies were severally known, lived in fairy forts and loved music and dancing but could be malicious if crossed. They could cause a person to lose their way; the person's only protection against this was to turn their coat inside out. Even cattle were not safe from the darts of the fairies. Prehistoric flint tools and weapons found in some areas were believed to be fairy darts that harmed cattle.

It was considered the height of folly to upset the fairy folk in any way. Illness, the death of cattle, a fire that could destroy a farmhouse – every and any sort of misfortune could follow such foolhardiness. Road workers would bypass a fairy fort lest they upset its supernatural inhabitants. When rural electrification was introduced in Ireland in the 1950s, engineers had to be careful that they did not run cables through or plant poles in certain ancient land-marks. Even to this day many a hard-headed farmer will refuse to allow a fairy thorn tree to be dug up on his land lest it bring him ill-luck.

Belief in the supernatural has been common in Ireland since before the dawn of history. This may be due to the fact that in Irish folklore there is little difference between the fairy world and the kingdom of the dead. Traditionally the fairies were said to be fallen angels. When God was ridding the heavens of rebellious angels, Saint Michael grew worried. He feared that the heavens would soon be emptied. He pleaded for mercy and God stayed his hand. Some angels had reached Ireland, where they remain to this day. Fairies are said to resemble human beings and each person has a fairy double for a guardian angel.

Treated with proper caution and respect, the Good People could be neighbourly. They were known to help hard-pressed farmers with the sowing of crops or to take a hand with the spinning and weaving. They might even help a poor man pay his rent by giving him a purse of gold (which, of course, turned into dried leaves in the grasping landlord's hand).

A popular legend tells of the merry fiddler who was born a hunchback. One night on his way home from a wake he wandered into a fairy fort and fell asleep. When he awoke the moon was high in the sky and the fort was now an elegant room with a ceiling of twinkling stars and a crescent moon. A crowd of fairy folk were dancing in a circle and singing the same song over and over again: '*Dé Luain, Dé Máirt, Dé Luain, Dé Máirt.*' In the end the little fiddler grew tired of the tune and decided to put a bit of *snas* on it. He drew out his fiddle, struck up and sang right merrily: *'Dé Luain, Dé Máirt agus Dé Céadaoin.'* ('Monday, Tuesday and Wednesday.')

The Good People were delighted, and to reward him they removed the hump from his shoulders before sending him home with a purse of gold. Now the fiddler's neighbour was another hunchback but without a note of music in his head. Small blame to him for that, only in addition he was as cantankerous as a bag of cats.

When he heard the story he determined to visit the fairy fort for himself, but if he did he was to rue the day. While the Good People were still dancing and singing he burst out in a voice so raucous as to make a crow wince, 'Wednesday, Thursday, Friday and Saturday.' So enraged were the fairies at the intruder's bad manners and lack of musical skill that they determined to teach him a lesson. He was lifted in the air and when he came down he saw with dismay that, far from having no hump, he now possessed two.

Leprechauns have been around these parts for thousands of years. They are reputed to be water spirits, kin to the shadowy Tuatha Dé Danaan, whose magic was no match for the iron weapons of the belligerent Celts when they first came to settle in Ireland around 500 BC. Leprechauns have always been portrayed as hard-working creatures, shoemakers by trade, lending a splash of colour to the countryside with their green jackets, red caps and white owl feathers. Furthermore they are associated with that marvel of nature, the rainbow, beneath the foot of which they hide their crock of gold.

There are many stories told in Ireland of how the leprechaun outwits a greedy human who wishes to rob him of his hard-earned crock. It is difficult to find a leprechaun, but if you do you must hold him fast. One account tells how a mean-minded woman succeeds in catching one. She shakes him by the coat until he points out where his gold is buried, under a certain bush. The trouble is that the field is filled with similar bushes. But the woman is no fool. She ties her garter around the bush in question and then goes home in search of a spade to dig up the crock of gold. When she returns, the leprechaun has vanished and every bush in the field has a garter tied around it, so that the woman is defeated and the leprechaun keeps his hiding place safe from mortal eyes.

The great pagan god Lugh is associated with leprechauns. He was the patron of shoemakers, and it is said that the little men can sometimes be glimpsed at Ardagh Hill – or to use its ancient name, Brí Leith – in County Longford, one of the most famous fairy seats in Ireland.

One of our earliest tales recounts how Eisirt, poet to the king of the leprechauns, came on a visit to Ireland. He ended up in the banqueting hall at Emain Macha, where he was mocked for his size, almost drowned in a bucket of wine, half-smothered in a pot of porridge and finally befriended by Aed, the High King's jester. Eisirt invites Aed back to the place known as Magh Faithlenn, 'home of the leprechauns'. Now and again, fishermen or children at play catch sight of that far-off island, but when they look again the place has vanished and the seas are empty. The story of Aed's visit, in the company of Eisirt, ends on a splendid note in the old tale:

Aed was nobly treated in the kingdom of the leprechauns, and after that he went back to the Palace at Emain Macha and wrote down in gold ink in *The Annals of*

Ulster the story of how Eisirt came to Ireland and all he could remember of Magh Faithleann, which lies off the west coast of Ireland and is the true home of the dwarves.

Now and again a child might be taken away by the fairies, and a changeling – a wrinkled, cross little man – left in the infant's cradle. The changeling loved music but was frightened of iron and fire. If either was brought near the cradle, the changeling would jump up and disappear out the door, to be replaced shortly by the stolen child.

Young brides were at risk on May Eve, when they could be abducted in the *sí gaoithe*, the 'fairy wind', which blew up without warning and swept mortals away. Slievenamon ('the Mountain of Women'), situated in County Tipperary in the Golden Vale and 2,364 feet high, overlooks five counties and has always been regarded as a magic mountain. Fionn Mac Cumhail lived there, as did his companions in the *Fianna* and fifty beautiful maidens, who gave the mountain its name. It is said that people who live around the foot of the mountain are touched by enchantment. In the closing years of the nineteenth century, a young man named Michael Cleary, who lived in Ballyvadlea in south Tipperary, became convinced that his wife was a changeling and that the only way he could banish the spirit and recover the wife he loved was by the ordeal of fire. So with the help of some neighbours he held the unfortunate woman above the grate and when her calico chemise caught fire she perished. The young husband and nine neighbours were taken to Clonmel jail and tried for murder, but the evidence was so conflicting and so bizarre – it was said that they lived in a fairy-haunted world – that they were treated leniently for the times that were in it. In the years that followed only five of the nine houses in the little village remained inhabited, the population halved and Michael Cleary had emigrated to Montreal.

Irish folklore abounds with stories of other supernatural creatures. One favourite was the Hag of Bears, said to be the oldest and wisest woman in Ireland. She could remember back to the Ice Age. Then there was Gerald the Rhymer, Fourth Earl of Desmond and Lord Chief Justice of Ireland in 1367. Tradition has it that he was swept away by the people of the *sí* and sleeps beneath the waters of Lough Gur in County Limerick, whence he emerges every seven years to ride the ripples of the lake. Another such person is the O'Donoghue of the Glens (Glenflesk in County Kerry), who is bound by spells to gallop over the Lakes of Killarney and doomed to continue his rides until the silver horseshoes of his mount wear out.

But by far the best-known figure in Irish folklore is the banshee (*bean sí*, or 'fairy woman'). Until recent times there was scarcely a person in Ireland who had not heard or caught glimpse of the banshee. She was known as the messenger of death − a weird and ghostly presence who might be seen cowering under a tree or perched on top of a house combing her hair. She wore a long dark cloak and her feet were never seen. Woe betide the unfortunate at whom she might fling her comb. Should it find its mark, that person was doomed soon to die.

Legends of death messengers can be traced back to pre-Christian Ireland. In the *Tain Bó Cuailgne*, we learn how when Cúchulainn sets

out to hold the Pass of Ulster against Queen
Maeve's army, he meets a beautiful woman
washing severed limbs and bloodied clothes at
Átha na Foraire on the plains of Emain Macha.
His druid warns him that the girl is the banshee
and that slaughter and death will follow his
stand. But Cúchalainn refuses to turn back. The
saga tells us that, when death was upon Cúchulainn, he caused himself to be bound to a
stone pillar so that he would die standing up.
After that the banshee came in the shape of a
crow and sat on his shoulder and the onlookers
knew that the great hero was dead.

A thousand years later the banshee, in the
form of the fairy queen, Aoibheall, appeared to
Brian Boru on the eve of the Battle of Clontarf
in 1014, at which the Vikings were put to flight,
to forewarn him that he would be killed on the
morrow. But the king chose to believe that
whatever was fated would come to pass. From
Aoibheall we move forward in time to the
middle of the seventeenth century, when the
banshee was given the name of Áine. Her
music, the *ceol sí*, was said to comfort the dying
and their families.

Not everyone could boast a banshee in the family. She haunted only the best families – whose offspring were born on the right side of the blanket – and especially those possessing the gift of music. The seventeenth-century Kerry poet Piaras Feiritéar satirised the merchants of Dingle when they claimed to have heard her wailing. 'They need not fear that the banshee would raise a lament for them,' he said scathingly. 'The cry they heard was for Maurice Fitzgerald, head of the great Norman family.' It was said that the Fitzgeralds had a special relationship with the banshee; they claimed her as an ancestor and gloried in this claim.

If a seriously ill person heard the banshee it was a sign that death was at the door. The tradition of the bansheee even spread to America, carried across the Atlantic by emigrants in the eighteenth, nineteenth and twentieth centuries. There too her appearance was considered something of a status symbol by the families she haunted.

While the pagan Irish believed in the here-after, the concept of hell was unknown to them. The dead went to *Tír na nÓg*, 'the Land of Eternal Youth', or to the old Irish Elysium,

Magh Meall, 'the Plain of Honey'. Hell is described in Irish tradition as a place not of fire but of freezing cold. The Irish did not take too kindly to the idea of eternal damnation, however, and the popular belief is that only one person was ever condemned to hell – the unfortunate Judas Iscariot, the betrayer of Christ.

5

IRISH HOSPITALITY

Irish hospitality was no myth but a reality – a tradition that goes back thousands of years and has lasted down to our times. In pre-Christian Ireland, to be considered miserly or niggardly or to refuse hospitality to any caller at the door was the greatest dishonour a person could bring upon himself. Later, Christian thinking dovetailed into the earlier pagan code, with its belief in the virtues of liberality towards the poor and needy, as well as obligations towards the guest.

Down the centuries visitors to our shores were astonished at the surpassing generosity of the Irish. Even the Viking marauders of the tenth century were affected by this. In the Icelandic sagas we find records of how the Irish built houses at crossroads in order to encourage passers-by to drop in and join them for a meal.

So impressed were these Norse pirates that when they got home they adopted the custom themselves. 'Is it leave the house with a curse upon it?' is still said in many parts if a visitor refuses food or drink.

Not only was the host expected to provide for his guest in early Ireland, but the fare must be the best the kitchen could produce. It was against all the laws of hospitality to economise on butter, even though that could be a scarce commodity during the winter months. This is borne out in an obituary notice in the *Annals of Ireland* under the date 1486: 'Neidhe O'Mulconry, head of the inhospitality of Ireland, died this year. He it was who solemnly swore that he would never give bread *and* butter to his guests.'

If Neidhe O'Mulconry has come down to us as the meanest man in Ireland, Buchet the Hosteller is remembered as the most generous. His story was first written down in the tenth-century *Yellow Book of Lecan* but is much more ancient than that; it was a favourite with storytellers down the centuries.

Buchet was a kindly and unselfish man whose hospitality was abused by the twelve profligate brothers of his dearly loved foster-daughter Eithne. The young men regularly came guesting with large companies of equally reckless and thankless fellows until all Buchet had left was seven cows where once there had been seven herds of cattle. Buchet was ruined and was forced to leave his fine hostel and move to a woodman's cottage at Kells, County Meath, near the fort of the noble Cormac, who had his sights set on the kingship of Ireland.

A year passed, and Cormac, now High King, was out riding in the forest when he came upon a beautiful young girl milking her cows. He stopped to admire her. First she skimmed the milk and put the cream in a special vessel, then she gathered rushes and tied the best in a special bundle and finally she waded into the middle of the stream to draw a pail of water.

The king was intrigued by this. 'Who are you, and why do you so carefully divide the cream and the rushes and draw the freshest water?' he demanded, reining his horse still nearer. She smiled at him and his heart turned over.

'I am Eithne, foster-daughter of Buchet,' she

said, 'and I give him the best I can, for he is the most generous man in the world and had I the power I would give him twice as much.'

Cormac sent a messenger to Buchet asking for Eithne as his concubine, but the hosteller gave an emphatic refusal. Like most young lovers the king was consumed with desire – besides, he was used to getting whatever he set his heart on. In a temper, he carried Eithne away to his *dún*, or fortress. She spent the night in his bed, and, as they say, the earth moved for both of them. Little wonder that on the same night she conceived a son. But she was worried about Buchet and returned to his cottage the following day.

Nothing could hold the king back now he had possessed Eithne. Within a week he had made her his queen and paid the bride-price to Buchet: all that the hosteller could see from the rampart of Kells – cows and men, oxen and horses, jewels, torcs and rings – so much in fact that Buchet could scarcely carry his wealth of herds and gold back to his former home.

Ever after, the story tells us, Buchet continued to keep open house to entertain as many guests as came. There was always food and drink in plenty and fifty musicians played so beautifully that, to this day, storytellers speak of the 'wonder of the melodies of Buchet's hostel'. And as for Cormac and Eithne, as in all the best stories they lived happily ever after, or so it is said.

In Irish tradition it was the custom to give the finest portion of any feast to the acknowledged champion or hero. Ten miles north of Newry on the main Dublin–Belfast road is the little village of Loughbrickland. Close by and sheltered by low hills and trees is Bricriu's Lake, which takes us back 2,000 years to one of the most famous stories in the Ulster cycle, 'Bricriu's Feast'.

In a poem in an old Irish manuscript that is held in the Bodleian Library at Oxford, it is said of Bricriu that 'A blister, big as a fist, would swell on his face if he knew some secret concerning an honest man and could not blab it out at once.' He knew everyone's weakness, for as he said of himself, 'Clearer to me is a whisper than a cry to anyone else.'

Bricriu Poison Tongue, as he was called, was the greatest troublemaker in Ulster and everyone groaned when they heard he was preparing a grand feast. Not only was he malevolent but he was sufficiently wealthy to indulge his whims. For the feast he had a special house built, modelled on the Red Branch Knights' palace at Emain Macha, with nine rooms overlaid with gold. By dint partly of wheedling and cajoling but mainly by threats he persuaded the king and his retinue to attend the feast.

At the high table Bricriu had prepared the champion's portion: a roast boar which had been sweetened on fine meal, milk curds, wheat and beef broth, a prime beef, a hundred wheaten cakes cooked in honey and other titbits too numerous to mention, all accompanied by the finest wine, ale and mead. Before long the three champions of the Red Branch Knights, Cúchulainn the Hound of Ulster, Leogaire the Truimphant and Conall Cernach the Victorious were at loggerheads as to who should sit in the place of honour.

Meanwhile, Bricriu went in search of the champions' wives: Fidelma, wife of Leogaire; Lendabair, wife of Conall Cernach; and Emer, wife of Cúchulainn. To each lady he whispered the same message: 'Whoever enters the dining room first shall prove her husband is champion and will take precedence over all the women of Ulster.'

Shortly afterwards the ladies made their way from their quarters to the great hall. At first they walked easily and gracefully, then they quickened their steps and finally they caught up their robes and broke into a run, so that they all reached the door together and fought for entrance. Their husbands were now at daggers-drawn. There would be no peace in Ulster until the matter was resolved.

In the midst of all the confusion a churlish giant of a fellow arrived demanding hospitality. In one hand he carried a chopping block and in the other an enormous sharp-edged axe. He announced to the company that he was seeking in Ulster what he could find in no other place – fair play. He proposed a test. He would cut off the head of the bravest warrior in the banqueting hall and return the following evening and allow his own head to be chopped off. When he found no takers he reversed his order: his head would be first, and the warrior's head would be chopped off the following night. They thought him mad, but he created such a fuss that in the end Leogaire the Triumphant took up the axe and clove the churl's head from his body. Whereupon the churl tucked his bloody head under his arm and marched off. On the following night he came back, with his head on his shoulders. But Leogaire was missing.

Next Conall Cernach the Victorious took up the challenge, and again the churl marched off carrying his head. When he reappeared on the second night Conall Cernach was nowhere to be found. Loud and sharp were the churl's words as he upbraided the company. Amongst other insults, he called them white-livered, knock-kneed cowards and swore there wasn't the leavings of a champion amongst the lot of them.

This was too much for Cúchulainn. He chopped off the churl's head with a mighty blow. The following night he was there waiting for doom to fall. He laid his head on the chopping block; with a grunt of satisfaction the churl tested the keenness of his axe and then, satisfied, swung it to the rafters. The sound it made coming down was like the rushing wind in a forest of trees on a stormy night and those in the hall held their breaths with fear. Cúchulainn felt the axe shave his hair but that was all. He rubbed his neck to make sure it was still where it belonged and then looked up to find the churl grinning down at him.

'Rise up, Cúchulainn,' the churl ordered. 'There is not a champion in Ulster or in all Ireland that can claim to be your equal in courage, in skill and in honour. I am of the Tuatha Dé Danaan and I swear by the magic of my people that if anyone challenges your right from this night on he shall die.' With that the churl vanished from the great hall, and never again at any feast or banquet was Cúchalainn's right to the hero's portion questioned.

Perhaps the best-remembered account of a banquet in the traditional manner is that of Brian O'Rourke, Prince of Bréifne, who at Christmastide in the year 1591 held 'open house' in the great hall of Dromahaire Castle, County Leitrim. The occasion was celebrated in the folk song 'Pléaráca na Ruarcach' ('O'Rourke's Revel Rout') and was immortalised by Dean Swift when in 1720 he translated the words of the song. The music of Pléaráca was composed by Turlought Carolan (1670–1738), the last and perhaps greatest of the Irish bards:

> O'Rourke's noble fare will ne'er be
>   forgot
> By those who were there and those
>   who were not,
> His revels to keep we sup and we
>   dine
> On seven score sheep, fat bullock and
>   wine.
>
> Usquebaugh to our feast in pails was
>   brought up
> A hundred at least, and a madder our
>   cup,
> Oh here is the sport, we rise with the
>   light
> In disorderly sort, from snoring all
>   night.

6

MYTHS AND LEGENDS

It was considered admirable in Irish folklore to be resourceful, and to be able to outmanoeuvre one's rivals was a mark of high intelligence. One of the cleverest characters in storytelling was a wily mason who could outwit anyone, friend or foe. A popular story about him goes as follows.

Once upon a time there lived in Ireland a master builder who was known as a *Gobán Saor*. Now one day the *Gobán* sent his son to the fair with a sheep – and instructions to bring back the animal and its price. The unfortunate boy was convinced his father had set him an impossible task. On the road, however, he met up with a young woman, to whom he told his sad tale.

'You can keep the sheep and I'll give you its price,' she said. 'It will be a fair bargain.' With that she took a pair of shears out of a bag and sheared the sheep of its wool. Then she gave the boy a golden guinea and sent him home with the shorn animal. The *Gobán* was pleased with the bargain and said, 'That girl is the wife for you' – a decision which was well received, for the young pair had fallen in love at first sight.

A year passed and the king sent for the *Gobán* to build him a new castle. 'I'll take you with me and teach you the trade,' the *Gobán* said to his son, 'if you shorten the road for me.'

'How can I do that?' the young man asked his wife that night in bed.

'By chatting him up and telling him stories,' she advised.

The *Gobán* and his son spent a year and a day working on the castle, and it's no lie to say it was a magnificent building. But the king was determined that its equal would never be built and planned to lock up the mason and his son as soon as the last brick was in place.

The *Gobán* guessed what was afoot and asked the king's son to fetch him a special tool from home which he needed to put the finishing touches to the tower. The tool, he said, was called 'Twist for Crookedness'. His daughter-in-law would know what he meant. Of course she did, and in turn she imprisoned the prince, sending word back to the king that she would 'exchange one for two'.

The king was no fool. He released his prisoners and gave them a bag of gold for their trouble. As soon as they arrived safely home, the young woman let the prince go free. After that the fame of the Gobán Saor and his clever daughter-in-law spread through the land.

Luck, good or ill, played a very important part in Irish folk tradition. It was believed that a child born with a caul (a skin covering a child's head at birth) would never drown. Sailors, like fishermen, are superstitious people because of their dangerous calling and were always prepared to pay handsomely for a caul. Another belief was that the seventh son of a seventh son was born with 'the cure', which meant he could treat people for a variety of illnesses. Then, too, there was a strong belief in the 'evil eye' and a curse that could follow a family for generations. The widow's curse was the most feared of all. A source of ill-luck could be a *geis*, or taboo, which would prevent a person from doing certain things, under pain of death.

'The Destruction of Da Derga's Hostel', which comes from oral sources and is found in *The Book of the Dun Cow*, tells of what happened when a High King of Ireland broke his *geasa*, or taboos. In those far-off days, Da Derga's Hostel was one of the four great houses of hospitality in Ireland where a traveller could stay without payment of any kind for as long as he or she wished. The hostel was situated at Bohernabreena ('the road to the hostel'), close to Tallaght and not far from the centre of Dublin.

Da Derga, who was admired for his long red hair and feared for his temper, was the confidant of King Conaire the Great, who had his court at Tara some time before the coming of Christianity. Now in King Conaire's reign there were three crowns of plenty on the land: fish in the rivers, oakmast up to the knees every autumn to fatten the pigs and ships in harbour unloading their cargoes of silks and wines in return for Irish hounds and gold, which were freely exported and much in demand. Men, women and children travelled the roads in safety, for in all the land amity and prosperity reigned. But nothing lasts forever, and in the end the peace was broken by the king's six foster-brothers, wild and reckless men who plundered and pillaged at will. He banished them from Ireland, and they and their followers turned to piracy, plundering the coasts of England, Scotland and Ireland.

As King Conaire was descended from the Tuatha Dé Danaan, or fairy people, certain things were forbidden him. To mention but a few, he could not go right-hand-wise round Tara and left-hand-wise round Magh Breg, he could not spend more than nine nights in a row away from his royal seat at Tara and three redheads should not go before him into the house of a red-haired man.

For a long time King Conaire was careful to keep his *geasa*, but in the end fate will catch up with king or commonor – though Conaire had no inkling on the day he set out on his mission of peace that his days were numbered. He was called south to settle a dispute between two rival chiefs and spent ten days making the peace, which meant he had broken his first taboo. On his return journey, when he crossed the borders of County Meath, he saw that the whole country around Tara was a sheet of flame and rolling smoke. He realised that in his absence his foster-brothers had sacked the palace and, to avoid an encounter, he broke two more of his taboos by going right-hand-wise round Tara and left-hand-wise round the plains of Brega.

He then turned south along the coast, crossed the River Liffey and decided that he would spend the night at the *bruíon,* or hostel, of his friend Da Derga. Near Bohernabreena he saw three red-haired horsemen and remembered his taboo that three redheads should not go into the house of a red-haired man before him. He sent his son with a request that they turn back, but they sped on, chanting, 'Lo, O prince, great the tidings. We ride the fairy horses of the *sidhe.* Though we are alive we are dead. Great the slaughter, ravens sating themselves with the blood of the dead.' A sense of doom came upon King Conaire and he gave a great sigh. 'All my *geasa* have seized upon me this night,' he said.

Meanwhile, his foster-brothers had left Tara and under cover of darkness had reached the foot of the Dublin hills. Speed and surprise were their allies when they reached Bohernabreena. Three times they set the hostel on fire and three times the flames were quenched by King Conaire, who was mortally wounded in the end. Druids who were with the fairy horsemen put the curse of thirst on the king. He asked for a drink of water but the flames had dried up the River Dodder, which rang through the great hall. And so died King Conaire. Outside there was no moon but the sky was no longer dark. It was slashed with crimson like a great river of blood. Then the walls fell down and thus was accomplished the destruction of De Derga's Hostel.

Animal tales are very old, not only in Ireland but all over the world. In most stories the fox is portrayed as the wily animal capable of outwitting all his fellow creatures, although sometimes he himself is bested. Once a fox caught a hen and was about to swallow her down when she managed to get out the words, 'Nobody should eat a meal without saying grace first', whereupon the fox opened his mouth to pray and the hen escaped. ''Tis only a fool would say grace until after he has eaten,' the fox said bitterly as he watched his dinner disappear down the road.

Another story tells of a man driving his cart to the market with a load of fish. He saw what he thought was a dead fox on the road, and, thinking the fur would come in useful, threw the animal into the back of the cart. But as soon as the man's back was turned, the wily fox came to life, and what it didn't manage to eat it carried home to its cubs.

Finally there is the story of a fox who met a crow with, in her mouth, a large and luscious cheese which she was carrying home to her nest. 'I hear tell you have the most beautiful voice in the world,' said the deceitful fox, 'and there isn't your equal for singing.' He sat at the side of the road, his head cocked, his mouth open, waiting. Sure enough the vain, foolish crow believed him and opened her mouth to croak, whereupon the cheese fell to the ground and the fox pounced and ate it up.

Legends were originally accounts of the lives of the saints and such works were usually read aloud in monasteries at mealtimes. Legends of course have also come to mean traditional stories. So we have folk legends, which may take the form of stories about ghosts or fairies, and legends about poets, highwaymen or national heroes like Dean Swift, the eighteenth-century dean of St Patrick's Cathedral, Dublin, who was famed for his satirical wit, and Daniel O'Connell, known as the 'Liberator', who achieved Catholic emancipation in 1829. Many stories are told of O'Connell's skill as a lawyer. He was also a legendary ladies' man, and in folklore it is said that if you threw a stone at any bush you would be sure to hit one of his offspring. Then there are stories associated with unusual happenings like the night of the Big Wind in the nineteenth century or historical legends about the Great Famine or the Hungry Grass (where people collapsed of hunger because they were walking on the grave of a Famine victim). There are also supernatural legends about the headless coach; these ghosts were usually associated with notorious landlords and were seen near their homes. The headless coach presaged death for the beholder.

The pagan Irish were used to the idea of Hy-

Brasil, or Tír na nÓg, where the rivers ran high with milk and honey as well as sparkling waters and birds and animals played their accustomed parts, as they do in life. This belief was carried over to the Christian era. Nearest of all to the hearts of the early hermits were the birds. We are told in a twelfth-century manuscript called the *Dinnshenchas* – a collection of legends in prose and verse that purport to explain the names of famous places, rivers, lakes and hills – that a flock of singing birds had welcomed Patrick to Ireland when he returned on his mission of conversion.

Of all the various legends, probably those that deal with the pets of the early Irish saints are the most attractive. In *The Book of Leinster* we find the story of three young monks who went to sea hoping to find a deserted island where they would spend their days in prayer and penance. They took with them three oaten cakes and some water. As they were leaving, the youngest begged to take his pet and, although his companions were austere men who had sworn to give up everything, they could not deny their brother monk.

So they cast away their oars and threw

themselves on the mercy of the Lord and in due
time were driven by a fair wind to an island with
plenty of water and firewood. There they built
a church. Their intention was to live on water-
cress and seaweed, but each day the little cat
went swimming in the sea and each evening it
returned, carrying a large salmon. And the three
monks were distressed and said, 'Oh God, our
pilgrimage is no hardship now. We brought no
provisions but our cat feeds us well.' An angel
appeared to them and told them it was God's
will that food should be provided for them.
They accepted the angel's message and lived to
a very great age.

Early Ireland was covered with deep woods
where hermits built beehive huts and lived in close
companionship with the creatures of the wild.
Saint Ciarán of Saigir, patron saint of the men of
Ossory, had as companions several animals he had
tamed: a fox, a badger, a wolf and a stag. They
lived together in peace and followed the wishes of
the saint in all things. But one day the fox fell from
grace and stole Ciarán's shoes, which were made
of the skin of a goat.

Ciarán sent the badger, who knew the ways

of the wild, in search of the fox, and the badger found that wily animal about to eat the shoes. The fox was dragged back to Ciarán by the scruff of the neck and the saint said, more in sorrow than in anger, 'Brother, why did you do this? It is unworthy of you. Our water is sweet and is common to all, likewise our honey and fruit and vegetables. Had you craving for flesh, the omnipotent God would have made the bark of the tree taste of such at our prayers. Then the fox begged forgiveness and fasted until commanded by Ciarán to eat. After that they all lived in harmony until God called them home.

Another lovely legend tells of Saint Mochua, a hermit who had given up all worldly goods save for a cock, a mouse and a fly. The office of the cock was to keep the hours of matins for Mochua and if he was likely to sleep longer than the five hours he allowed himself, the mouse would awaken him by licking his ear. The fly's business was to act as a bookmark and walk along each line of the psalter as Mochua read it and remain at the line until the saint returned again to the singing of the psalms.

Bees and honey were considered so important

in Ireland that a whole chapter is devoted to them in the brehon laws, which were in force from pagan days down to the sixteenth century. It was commonly believed that if a member of the family died, the bees in the garden should be the first to be told, otherwise they would take umbrage and set up their hives elsewhere.

Honey and mead played a part in the fare of the early monks. The coming of the first swarm of bees to Ireland is attributed to Saint Madomnoc, who lived in the sixth century and is patron of Tibberaghny and Fiddown in County Kilkenny.

As a young man, Madomnoc went to a monastery in Wales to study with the great Saint David, where his special care was beehives, which formed part of the abbey's wealth. Now when the time came for Madomnoc to return home, the bees refused to be parted from him. Three times they followed him to the ship waiting to set sail for Ireland, and three times he bore them back to their hives. In the end, Saint David generously presented the swarm of bees to his protégé and disciple with the words, 'May the land to which you are brought abound with your progeny and may their species and generation never fail, but our own foundation shall be deprived of you.'

According to the legend, Madomnoc set up a foundation at Fingal, near Balbriggan, which bore the name 'the Church of the Beekeepers', The bees prospered and multiplied there, but none were afterwards found in the monastery of Menevia in Wales, where Saint David ruled. Lovers of bees and honey might like to know that Saint Madomnoc's feast day falls on 13 February.

If Saint Madonmoc is credited with the introduction of bees to Ireland, Saint Gobnait of Ballyvourney is regarded as the patron saint of beekeepers. Like Madomnoc, her feast day is in February and she too is reputed to have lived in the sixth century. The legend tells us that she was renowned for the honey her bees produced. Honey was valuable in those days and she bartered her stock for flour, meat, milk and oats, which she distributed to the poor. Thus she brought prosperity to the people until an invading chief and his army descended on Ballyvourney with plunder and rapine in mind. But they

reckoned without Gobnait, who, like the great
Saint Brigid, was a redoubtable woman, used to
getting her way. She prayed for guidance and
was inspired by the Holy Spirit to let loose her
bees. According to some accounts, the bees
turned into soldiers and routed Gobnait's en-
emies, but a more likely scenario is that the
enraged bees, on Gobnait's instructions, stung
the marauders so badly that the cowardly fellows
fled for their lives. Their work done, the bees
dutifully returned to the hive and the making of
honey.

But perhaps the most appealing legend of all
was one that was once common all over Ireland.
It was written down from oral sources by Giraldus
Cambrensis – Gerald the Welshman – who
visited the island in the twelfth century to
compile the first travel book about Ireland. The
legend tells how a certain priest set out one
night to tend a dying man, taking with him the
Sacred Host. A swarm of bees came his way
and, forgetting his errand, he laid the Host
down on the grass and, gathering up the bees,
went home.

The little creatures left him, however, and

went back to where the Host lay in a greensward and bore it away. Deep in the woods they made a chapel of fair wax, a chalice of wax and a waxen priest and paid reverence to the Host. The legend relates how, after much searching, the priest found that which he had lost and was astonished and asked God for forgiveness for his neglect. After that many people, including the sick man who had recovered miraculously, came to the woods to see the marvel and praised God for the work of the bees.

Select Bibliography

Cahill, Thomas. *How the Irish Saved Civilisation*. London, 1995.

Dillon, Myles. *Early Irish Literature*. Chicago, 1948.

Flower, Robin. *The Irish Tradition*. Oxford, 1947.

Lysaght, Patricia. *The Banshee*. Dublin, 1986.

Mahon, Bríd. *Land of Milk and Honey*. Dublin, 1998.

Mahon, Bríd. *While Green Grass Grows*. Dublin, 1998.

Mahon, Bríd. *The Wonder Tales of Ireland*. Dublin, 1976.

Ó Catháin, Séamus. *The Festival of Brigit*. Dublin, 1995.

Ó Duilearga, Séamus. *Leabhar Shéain Í Chonaill*. Dublin, 1948.